About the author

Born in Germany shortly before WWII, Edith Polski had already married and divorced before migrating to Australia in 1970 with her daughter. She worked in an office in Sydney for three years before remarrying and moving to the New South Wales North Coast.
After another divorce, she continued to live on her bushland property for 17 years, with her daughter and grandchildren for neighbours. In 2002 she moved out of isolation to live near her sister in town.
Today, Edith writes, cares for her many pets and concentrates on her hobbies.

This Life

Edith Polski

❧

National Library of Australia Cataloguing-in-Publication entry
Polski, Edith, 1935- author.
This life / Edith Polski.
ISBN 9780646934372 (paperback)
Subjects: Polski, Edith, 1935-
Germans—Australia—Biography.
Self-analysis (Psychoanalysis)
Self-actualization (Psychology)
Spiritual life.
920.720994

PAPER
HORSE

Design & Typesetting by Paper Horse Design & Publishing
Set in Adobe Minion Pro 11/14pt

Cover: Kuehrstedter Wald, 1980 photograph by the author

I dedicate the contents of my book to all those who are seekers of knowledge and who are looking for answers to better understand their lives.

Contents

1. Restless

For most of my life I was searching for something outside myself. I was hoping for better things to come: expecting people to be different, and had illusions about how things were supposed to be. This caused a feeling of longing for something that never came. This caused frustration; a feeling of general dissatisfaction within me that would never go away.

I wanted beautiful surroundings, dreamt of living in an elegant home, wearing fashionable clothes. I wanted to be beautiful, as I saw myself as ugly and fat. I had very low self-esteem. Any praise received I cast off as flattery, and trusted no one who tried to make me realise that I looked good.

When a decision had to be made I would ask close friends what they would do in my situation. Their attempts to help me increased my insecurity and confused me even more. These were nightmarish times, when I felt helpless, but somehow always got out of them. In the company of strangers, I was withdrawn and timid, as I was afraid to say something wrong, or that someone would laugh at me. It was difficult for me to enjoy myself, unless I had had a glass of wine or two, then I would loosen up. Music, also, would lighten my mood.

But nothing really fulfilled me. There was something missing in my life. I was searching but did not know for what. I knew from inside of me that there was more to life than I was living and experiencing. My belief was limited. I could not believe in God, or the Bible, as no one could tell me who had written the first page of it. Who had been the witness to see God creating the world and Adam and Eve?

But I knew for certain and strongly believed that there was a greater power than man. I called it Nature. Nature was stronger than any human construction. Its power was awesome: it could strike with unstoppable might and was to be respected, even feared.

I don't remember having any special dreams, then, and probably wouldn't have made much of it if I did, as I just didn't concern myself with esoteric matters. No one I knew ever talked about these matters. Or wasn't I listening?

The material world with its ups and downs was all around me. I lived as happily and as well as I knew how. I had been brought up with moral guidelines, chiefly the Ten Commandments, which kept me safe within my limited circle of family, friends and work colleagues. Aspirations for higher learning had been stifled long ago. The daily duties at work and home consumed all strength and time. There were no dreams, just a silent longing for something. But what?

This longing created an emptiness within, a feeling of loss in situations when problems arose. Who was I to turn to? Who would give support, encouragement? Who was to be trusted with my most secret inner needs? The feeling of standing alone in front of a mountain of problems, where I could see no way out, sent me to despair and hopeless unhappiness. Days like that were draining all my energy, crying myself to sleep, but life went on. Most times I found a solution overnight, never thinking that this solution might have come from a higher source.

I was married but felt dissatisfied and unhappy in the relationship, overburdened with responsibilities, exhausted and frustrated. I felt misunderstood, misjudged and misinterpreted. I did defend myself, but mostly in anger, when I couldn't see any other way. Before my anger erupted, I usually didn't say anything, because I knew if I opened my mouth this would be misunderstood again. Communicating my thoughts wasn't my strength. I had been accused too often of saying the wrong things at the wrong time, which made me reluctant to give my opinion freely, face to face.

It was a big step when I finally moved out of the family home and started out on my own with my four-year-old daughter. Some of the responsibilities were still there. I had to work. I had to look after my child, but there was support available to me from my parents, my employer and also from new friends, who accepted me into their neighbourly circle. It was new to me to live in a harmonious atmosphere.

But I still struggled for balance in my life, despite my new circle of friends. Loneliness and despair crept in at times when I could not see any use in living. So, one day, I tried to kill myself. Fortunately, my landlady found me in time and rushed me to hospital, where I could be saved.

It was a long road back to normality before I found hope again. The pain I had caused to family and friends made me feel guilty, but their love and concern made me aware that life was worth living.

Some time later, when the clouds had subsided, the opportunity arose, through my job, to fly to Rome for the day. That was an experience I would not forget easily. My first flight: I walked on the clouds, both actually and symbolically!

Seeing Rome was a sensation, so unexpected but so very much appreciated. My boss had asked the secretary in the

Rome office to take the day off and show me as many sights as was possible in the short time available.

One of the representatives was driving the car through the seemingly unorganised traffic as fast as he could. It was a warm spring day, the 28th February, 1968. People were sitting on The Spanish Steps in the sun. The coffee shops had windows and doors wide open, where we drank coffee in tiny cups amidst big bags of unburned coffee beans. I threw coins into the Fontana di Trevi. These are still in there, promising that one day I might return. I saw many beautiful historic buildings and places, including the Vatican, and had a delicious typical Roman meal in a cosy restaurant.

At the end of all the sightseeing, I bought a beautiful dress for my little girl before they rushed me back to the airport in the evening.

It was breathtaking and very emotional to watch a sunset over Rome from the plane, and it brought tears to my eyes. I clung to the small bunch of violets I had collected, bringing them, and new hope, home with me to a wintery Hamburg.

This experience changed my attitude towards life: I wanted to enjoy life more than I had before. I joined a travel club and soon, trips to the US were advertised at very reasonable prices. My divorce was finalised, from which I received a payout. This provided me with the funds for a holiday.

I took the chance and asked my girlfriend in California whether I could visit her. My friend replied in a telegram that I would be welcome, even though she was pregnant with her second child. I took this offer without hesitation. The thought of getting out into the world, flying again, meeting people, was wonderful to me. My parents were looking after my daughter for the four weeks.

Flying over that vast country with its mountain ranges, gorges, rivers and towns was very exciting. Finally, we landed in San Francisco, where I was picked up by my friends.

Even though distances restricted certain excursions during the days, as my friend did not drive, on weekends and evenings I was taken about to all the most interesting sights around this beautiful city. I felt comforted and spoiled as an honoured guest, and enjoyed my stay there tremendously.

My friend's small boy of four years taught me conversational English, which he could speak better than I. It was amazing what that did for me, helping me over the barrier of doubt into actually speaking.

The weather was also a healer to my grey weather mind from Hamburg. The sky was blue every day, with hot summer temperatures.

I learned to know some of the ways American people live and work, which seemed to me in many ways more free than I was used to, but also more restrictive in security. There was a problem with racism, which was evident and sadly noticed by me. But I saw many a sign written on cars or billboards which said: "America, Love it or Leave it."

I loved it for its vastness, and the beauty I had perceived during my short stay; for the freedom I could feel in the wide highways, the distances, the opportunities that people might create if they were willing to work hard.

This was a holiday which shone only the good light on all for me. Like Alice in Wonderland, I felt confident and free. I had fallen in love with a country, its way of life and a dream of a man, but this man was married and had two little children. When my holiday ended, I hoped the distance which lay between us would end the infatuation.

Letters followed me home though, pleading, and finally I

gave in to this affair which fulfilled my romantic notion of how love could be. I experienced a period of utter joy and happiness which lasted only eleven days. Even though I knew it was over for good, as circumstances weren't on my side, the following months I lived in the clouds. Eventually, I woke up to reality, and the decision that I wanted to start a new life with a man of my own.

A search for a substitute is futile when the heart is somewhere else. It took a while until I replied to an ad from another country. A relationship started, via correspondence, and led me to emigrate with my daughter to Australia, in 1970.

Many things changed. I moved to another country, away from family and friends, where I had to make my own decisions, and circumstances were harsher and different. I had to change my attitudes in many ways, but felt quite comfortable with it after I did.

Life with the new man in my life, whom I married later on, went smoothly, and both my daughter and I felt comfortable with him, our new surroundings and new-found friends. Learning the language properly was a challenge, and working in an office there brought minor problems, but all could be managed in time. We enjoyed living in Australia: the city, the beaches, the parks were all so inviting, and we learned to adjust fairly quickly.

My daughter had a difficult time ahead of her. She was seven years old and had been to school in Germany, but she could not speak any English. She was a very tall girl with a short haircut, and the children in the Balmain School, where she was placed in Kindergarten, did not believe she was a girl. She told us that they forced her to take her underpants off in the toilet. From then on we let her hair grow. My daughter learned to speak English without an accent, and she went through all the classes and finished high school. At first we had to help her, by speaking only English at home, so she could more easily adjust. That might be the reason that, today, she hardly ever speaks German and doesn't want to read it.

We wanted to find a house to live in, but we weren't financially secure enough to buy one. We found a block of land further north, which was accessible to us. We decided to live in the bush and began anticipating the challenges that it would bring. Travelling there on weekends or holidays kindled our ideas of living on a big property, doing some gardening and farming.

On one of those trips, we were involved in a head-on collision. This set us back, due to loss of wages. Friends in Sydney, and family from Germany, helped. While my job was secure, my husband couldn't continue at his work because of his injuries. He had to find a job that suited him better, and it took a while until we were back on our feet. Finally, we got a financial payout from the crash and could consider the planned move to the bush. Most of our physical injuries had healed, but my psychological phobia had not. I was frightened to travel in a car and was a menace to drivers.

More challenges were waiting for us when we moved to the country, to live alternatively, in November 1973. Very practical, down to earth methods were needed. I brought the knowledge I had from childhood, when we had lived in a farming area for two years, to the foreground, and forgot about the elegant things I had once wished for. I also enjoyed living in, and with, nature and animals. I freed myself even more from former beliefs.

On weekends, we had built a simple hut and established some water storage, but our sleeping and living quarters were in a big house tent that we set up on a clearing we had cut out ourselves. All our furniture and belongings were stored in big boxes in the tent. Our kitchen was in the hut, where we had also a table and chairs on an earthen floor, and had built some shelves for storage. Later on, we built an oven for cooking, which looked more like a barbecue. In time, we bought a second hand combustion stove that would be better for baking and cooking.

It had been our aim to build a house during that first year, but the cost of clearing the land, plus our living expenses, used up all of our accident payout. My husband then found a job as carpenter in a neighbouring town, 100 km away. It was a long trip there and back every day. Later on, he was offered a bed overnight, so that he did not have to drive home every day. I stayed home alone with my daughter. A helpful neighbour took Martina, together with her children, to school. She had a bicycle to ride down to their property. After one year, the carpentry business folded and all the employees lost their jobs. My husband could not find another job in the area. He tried to establish his own workshop, but it was difficult without electricity, and the fact that we lived so far out in the bush.

In 1974, my parents and Martina's father invited her to visit them in Germany during the school holidays. We still had our friends in Sydney, where we could stay if we visited there, and they helped to bring Martina to the airport. Martina often stayed at their place with their children during school holidays. Also, from the correspondence school, she had had several holiday stays in Sydney with other children from other parts of NSW. When Martina came back from Germany, she didn't want to speak English. She had enjoyed her holiday very much.

At the end of 1975, my parents came to visit. We lived in very primitive conditions in the bush and were still struggling to establish a sort of living there. They had difficulty understanding us. Their suggestions were meant well, but they did not appreciate our financial situation. My father's suggestions caused very angry opposition from my husband, and it became impossible for my parents to stay on. They went to Sydney, where they were taken in by their friends, who had a big house with room to spare for them. My daughter and I followed over the Christmas holidays. Later on, my friends helped me to rent a flat in Leichhardt where we could all live. My father wanted me to learn to drive a car and he paid for lessons. Unfortunately, I did not know the difference between an automatic and a manual car. When I got my licence, I still could not drive a manual car, which was what my husband had. I looked for a job and had some interviews, which might have been successful, but when my parents left in February, I went back home to my husband.

Unfortunately, my parent's holiday and stay, and subsequent early return, caused them difficulties with their finances, of which I was not aware. The stress about their holiday and the trouble financially brought on a heart attack in my mother, from which she eventually recovered.

I still got paid child endowment by Martina's father, and had a bank account in Germany. At the end of 1978, I took the chance to visit my parents in Germany. Martina stayed with her step-father, as they got along fine. Our relationship had mended somewhat, but there was still an underlying problem between us concerning my parents. On and off we had times when we did not speak and, because of this, I asked the government to pay me my share of unemployment benefit separately. This worked much better. I could oversee my own finances and we split the expenses. I learned then to control what was going on and where my money was spent.

There were times when we lived apart for weeks and didn't talk to each other. We also had one physical fight, which ended in a mutual agreement that this was not the life either of us wanted to live.

My husband's father, who had lived many years in Queensland but had gone back to die in Germany, lived in a retirement home there. He often sent money to his son, which helped with new equipment and materials.

My husband was the happy builder of sheds for animals, temporary buildings for us to have a little more comfort and a small house on the hill. He wasn't allowed to build the four bedroom mansion, on the other side of the property, with the second-hand material he had collected.

He had built a big shed to start a carpentry business, but it had no electricity, or water. He also built a garage, which included a bathroom and laundry. He built one building after the other, but he never really got around to finishing them off properly, or getting a permit for them. We had a lot of problems with white ants, and he would often just give up what he was working on and start a new one.

At the end of 1979, cheap flights became available and my husband took the opportunity to see his father in Germany. He arrived a day too late: his father had died suddenly, so he had to arrange the funeral and clean out his belongings. My friends in Germany helped him with the arrangements, and also let him stay at their place. Later on, he also visited my parents in Hamburg and stayed with them. My parents were surprised how nice and relaxed my husband could be away from the property. This was the man I had known in Sydney: he had been interested in communication, was intelligent, read and knew a lot and had been a good friend to my daughter and husband to me. The land, and his wild ideas of being Superman, had made him a stressed and hyper-active individual, who could explode from one minute to another. One doctor later on told me that he might be schizophrenic.

Fences were mended with my parents during his stay in Hamburg before my husband returned home to Australia. At home he continued in his usual way, with much the same result as before. We had a huge garden with many fruit trees, but could never make a living out of it. We had our own vegetables, eggs, some meat from rabbits and ducks, and geese we kept, but could never make any profit. There was too much work and too many costs for us. We also had our own milk, butter and some cheese, and lived fairly healthily, but there was plenty of work to do for all of us.

With the years, I lost interest in keeping animals and slaughtering them for food. We gave up having geese, ducks and rabbits. Killing the ones I had raised, with so much love and care, just conflicted with my feelings for them. I couldn't eat their meat any longer. Our cows suffered from the lack of good grass on our land, and the calves we had tried to rear suffered due to our inexperience. They stayed small and did not grow properly, despite the feed that we bought for them. One after the other, we learned that this land was unsuitable for cattle, so we gave them to another farmer who had plenty of good grass to keep them.

Friends from Sydney turned up one day and brought us two milking goats, which was another disaster for us. They started eating what we wanted to grow, and we did not have the fences needed for them. Finally, we gave them to a farmer who kept goats. That problem was solved.

Martina had always wanted a horse. She got one for free that was destined for the slaughterhouse. It was in poor condition and stayed that way, despite our feeding it well. It was an old horse, but she had one, and enjoyed having her Bob.

We had many visitors over the years from Sydney, and also from Germany.

Some visits were happy, others weren't so successful. The reason was often our simple lifestyle; the lack of the comforts of city life.

In 1980, my daughter's father died, aged 54. Martina and I flew to Germany. He had left his house to his daughter, so we stayed for three months and enjoyed visiting family and friends. When the house was sold, Martina bought a property near ours. She married very soon after and moved over there.

On Australia Day, 26th January, 1984, our friends from Sydney visited us and took us sightseeing in their car around the beautiful Great Lakes. On a curve, another driver ran into our car, which caused another head-on collision. There were injuries to all passengers. My husband was the least injured and drove home with a passer by to get his car. We were transferred in an ambulance to Taree hospital, where we were picked up by my husband later.

Due to Medicare, we received very good treatment for our injuries and had no financial difficulties, as we had had after our accident in 1972. Some of my injuries, which had been caused by the first accident and had not been properly treated, were attended to in a good professional way.

At the end of 1984, my parents visited again. We had the small cottage finished and made comfortable, but no water connection. We had electricity by then. We had a fully equipped kitchen in a newer building, which my husband had started while I was in Germany. But this house was also built without a plan: it was too small, too close to the boundary and ill-planned.

For six weeks our living together went peacefully. We went for drives and had some fun times. But then, one day, in the middle of the mulberry harvest, my husband turned against my father and wanted to kill him.

My husband threw pieces of wood at him, hitting him in the chest. My father was on blood thinning medication and in danger of bleeding to death. We had no telephone then, but people along the road did, though it was a long walk. The ambulance came and took my father to the hospital in Newcastle.

My parents moved in with my daughter and her husband. They lived on a neighbouring property 10 minutes walk away. They quickly extended their house, adding another large room where my parents could live. The work was done by my son-in-law, his friends and my father. It was nicely lined and painted, with windows and doors.

The fight between my father and husband was very destructive, mentally as well as physically. I continued doing my jobs, picking mulberries for hours a day and making juice. Sometimes my mother came over to help me, because my husband had no animosity towards my mother. One day, though, we had a fight and I threw a pair of secateurs at him, which pierced him on the wrist. He went to hospital straight away to stop the bleeding, and the word soon got around town. I seemed to have some friends in town, because they asked him what he had done to me. When he came back, he poured petrol into the window of his newly built kitchen, while I was in there making juice. He wanted to burn me alive.

I did not wait until he put the match in. We contacted the police and, under their supervision, I had to pack my belongings and move out. I did not want to move, as I knew possession of property is always more effective than owning it on paper. For security reasons, I had to leave and moved my things into the extension at my daughter's home, all packed up in boxes.

I was completely destroyed, and couldn't understand anything any longer. I went bush, walking for hours in the dark, as I had done so many times before when my husband and I had had arguments. Many nights I had been out in the bush and knew my way around. But my leaving made everybody worried. When I finally returned, my father blew up at me that I should consider my mother. I came to my senses, then, and settled down in a small caravan, which I had bought a short while before. It had been moved over to my daughter's place, close to the house, so I also had electricity.

The fight had endangered my father's health and ended our marriage there and then. My father had been lucky to get very good treatment at the Mater Hospital. The doctors there gave him a very thorough check-up, which resulted in him not needing to be on blood-thinning medication any longer. They changed his medication, but also found out that he had a leaking valve near his heart and wanted to operate on it. He refused and never had it done.

My parents flew home before Christmas that year. We all accompanied them to the airport. Bill and Martina made a flying trip in the car, and I flew with them from Williamstown to Sydney.

Even though we never talked about it, I assumed that my parents could see that the plans or ideas my husband followed were leading nowhere, except into difficulties or ruin. My father must have pointed this out to my husband, creating opposition in him, which he showed in very destructive anger towards me and my parents.

My husband stayed on the property. I applied for a housekeeper's job and live-in position in Sydney. A wealthy couple living in Rose Bay, originally of German background, employed me. I felt fenced in from 7 am to 7 pm, though I did get a long afternoon break. They were nice people, but city life with the noise and traffic did not make it easier for me to learn to drive. I just could not cope, despite the driving lessons my employer paid for. We finally came to an agreement that her daughter would drive her to wherever she had to go, while I took the bus or walked to do the shopping. Nero, her silvery poodle, was happy to accompany me whenever I walked to pick up the mail, go to the bank or do the local shopping. However, this lady was elderly and she needed a housekeeper who could drive. City life did not agree with me. I missed the country, the fresh air and my freedom and, no matter how much this lady offered me, because she wanted to keep me, I needed to go home. I helped out for a few months, on and off, while another housekeeper was found and then I left. We had become friends.

In 1985, the court awarded a payout for injuries incurred in the second collision. I used the money to come to an agreement with my husband over ownership of the property.

The property was valued and I was prepared to pay him half his share. We went to our solicitor together and signed an agreement, that I had prepared myself as I knew my way around a little about legal matters from my profession as an articled clerk. My husband then packed his belongings and moved away to the house he had bought. A few months later we were divorced.

Staying by myself on the land, fighting for myself, made me more confident, but it was still a struggle. All the unfinished buildings were still there, but there was no proper house for me.

I started cleaning away some of the hoarded treasures of my ex, piling them up in the unregistered old station wagon he had left behind and learning to drive up and down the hill at the same time. My son-in-law also came, with his truck, and together we collected five large truckloads of rubbish and dumped it on the tip. All the wooden material we burned on heaps. After all the work was done, the place looked quite tidy. I felt more confident with driving, too, learned to park between two trees and was happy about my progress. Then the gearbox in that old car broke. That was the end of my driving experience.

A kind neighbour contacted a former builder in town, who liked to do jobs in his spare time, especially if they were out in the open and in the bush. He was willing to finish the building my husband had started as best as he could, even though there was no building permit for it. His fee was very reasonable, but I had to pay for all the materials. My son-in-law suggested that the building should be pulled down and a new building started, with permit and all formalities. Today, I know, I should have taken his advice, but I did not then because I doubted that I could pay for a new house. Jack did the best he could. He made some conditions, though: the house needed a plan, which I drew, and many previously built parts had to be replaced with new materials and brought up to standard. The roof, the windows, the electrics, the plumbing, the septic, the outside walls and the verandah floorboards all needed proper attention.

To pay for all this work, I went back to work as a housekeeper, only coming home every second weekend for some months. When I was home, I was Jack's handyman, helping with carrying, painting and whatever was needed, including providing music from my cassette recorder.

Watching the building change into a proper house over the next few years, it made me realise what my home meant to me, being free and independent, and the owner of a 25 acre property.

I was always interested in studying, so in 1985 I enrolled in another correspondence course, for English and German for an HSC. As I was working as a housekeeper in Sydney, my time for studying was limited, but I could join the tutorials for German at the university and meet other students. There I met two friends who had enrolled in the same course, one from Munich, the other from England.

Ilona, from Munich, invited us for a cup of coffee. We got talking. Ilona had learned Astrology and wanted to do our horoscopes. We three had an instant rapport and it continued from then on. Debbie, from England, had a little daughter, who stayed with me for a week once, later on.

Ilona and I met several times in Sydney at her home, where I also met her husband. They were a very loving couple, accommodating and open-minded. I spent many days with them, enjoying their harmonious environment and encouragement. Ilona fostered my development in spiritual matters. She saw something in me that I did not. She kindled a flame in me to find out more, but she couldn't convince me then to start learning astrology. The time wasn't right.

In 1986, my sister came for a visit from Germany to stay with me. The accommodation on my land was still primitive, because the improvements to my house were moving very slowly. I lived in a very isolated spot, and my sister wanted to see more of the area. Friends took us sightseeing. Soon, she met a German man in a bigger town, through an agency, and fell in love. A few months later, they were married and she moved into his home. She never went back to Germany on her return ticket.

At the end of 1987, my parents also migrated to Australia, following my sister, leaving family and friends in Germany behind. My mother never got over the loss and was very homesick, even though she learnt English and tried to be positive. They wanted to live with me in the country. My house had been finished from the outside, but inside there was much that could be improved upon. I moved back into the cottage on my land and left the main house to my parents, but my parents were restless. They felt they were intruding on my life, especially as we had to share the kitchen and bathroom.

My father was eager to better the situation, using their own money. I knew I wouldn't be able to pay it back soon and was very worried about it. My parents visited my sister on and off, and my mother sometimes stayed behind to enjoy my sister's company a little longer. When I was alone with my father, I felt inhibited and had some difficulties getting along with him.

I had idolised my parents in many ways, but was also dissatisfied with them, because of how they had interrupted my higher education when I was young. This had created a blockage in me ever since that time. When they came to live with me in the new country, I could not understand them any more, because I had changed. I had great difficulty living with them, especially my father, who would criticise me, my surroundings and my circumstances. I took all of this to heart. I hadn't learned not to react, especially as it was meant well from his side.

While my mother was staying with my sister for several days, and I was alone again with my father, I tried to commit suicide for the second time. I took tablets and went bush, wandering around: where, I don't remember. I eventually found my way back home and just lay down to sleep, but fell into a coma. My father called the ambulance and I recovered in the local hospital. Later, I realised how much I had terrified my family and friends again. They were all so comforting and loving to me.

While I was in hospital, my sister rang Ilona and accused her of putting things into my head that didn't belong there. Ilona was shocked, but my decision to take the tablets had nothing to do with Ilona.

My parents then made the decision that my bathroom should be tiled and the house painted. They paid for it all; my father painted the house while I worked again as a housekeeper in Sydney for some months.

By then, I had applied at the Council for a permit for my house. After thorough inspection, I was granted one.

A flat in the neighbourhood of my sister's place became available, so my parents decided to move there, to be close to amenities and transport. I moved back into my home, but still worked on and off as a housekeeper in Sydney.

2. Changes

Life for me changed when I started to think about it differently. A friend had given me a hint, while discussing a problem with her, that it was most important to be true to oneself.

This idea was new to me and, at first, I did not understand what she meant. I had been brought up to be nice and considerate towards others. It had been customary in my family to be accommodating to other members of the family, friends and neighbours, even to the point of sometimes making it uncomfortable for ourselves. This had been my conditioning, which I continued, and handled my connections with others the same way.

It suddenly dawned on me that I had never really considered my own wishes or needs first. I was denying myself to myself. No wonder this had caused regrets and resentments within me later on.

Suddenly, I understood why I had difficulties expressing my inner feelings, and always kept them to myself. This had made me very unhappy, often to the point of despair. Communication with the very people who were closest to me had sometimes been strained due to my withdrawal, or sudden outbursts of anger. This had confused them, as well as myself. My nerves had been on edge. A walk in the bush, away from everything, usually gave me time and space to come to my senses.

This was going to change now: I wanted to be true to myself and base all future decisions on this notion.

Something new turned up with a book that had been left behind in the housekeeper's room in which I had stayed. John van Auken's *Past Lives and Present Relationships* kindled my interest in esoteric matters, which were foreign to me at that time. After that, I borrowed a small book on self-hypnosis and tried to hypnotise myself. It was easy to follow the given instructions and I could relax completely while looking at a designated point for a few moments. I was amazed that this could happen. It was great to relax so completely for five minutes, because these sessions only lasted that long.

Due to the two head-on collisions in ten years, in which I had been injured, my fear of being driven in a car had become detrimental. Something had to be done about it.

In 1987, my friend, Ilona, tried to help me and referred me to her doctor, who used hypnotherapy to heal phobias. He introduced some positive instructions in his surgery and handed me a cassette for practising at home. I listened to it twice a day. These positive suggestions helped, with the common-sense notion that fear itself attracts that which we fear. The advice given was sound and I followed it. This eased the tension in me.

My sister had found a doctor who had given up general practice to cure people with alternative methods, like hypnotherapy. As I had already learned that this method is helpful, I also went to this doctor for treatment. He made me sit in front of a TV screen, where I could see myself. He made me look at myself, and asked me why I hated myself so much? Until then I hadn't been aware of hating myself.

Music was his prescription, along with positive suggestion, which I listened to with headphones in his practice. At home, I continued to listen to his cassettes twice a day. He also gave me a mantra to recite often, which was:

"Every day, in every way, I'm getting better and better.
I have peace; I feel great; I am strong; I'll be free."

One day I began to see colours from my third eye during meditation. The beautiful colour of a glittering golden-green, oval-shaped picture in front of my closed eyes made me feel ecstatic.

When I asked this doctor to go one step further, to hypnotise me to find out about my past lives, he declined because that was not his aim.

During this time many things were happening around me that brought changes to my daily routine and lifestyle. These changes forced me out of the isolation of living in the bush, on selected days during the week. An opportunity arose for me to do a course in astrology in a neighbouring town.

This course connected me with a group of like-minded people, for lectures and discussions on the subject. As modern astrology is linked to psychology, there were often mentions of reincarnation. Learning astrology means learning about oneself, getting to know oneself: with all one's faults, difficulties and opportunities. The chart is a blueprint for life, with all its ups and downs, and positive opportunities that one is free to choose from.

This taught me a lot about myself and others. Suddenly, I could see myself differently. It broadened my horizon to focus on other people's needs, after I had read their charts; it gave me greater understanding as to why some people have such a hard time overcoming their stresses and strains.

It was during these months that I picked up some library books from a shelf in a different section. One was: *Soul Search* by Glen Williston & Judith Johnstone, and *The Other Side—an Account of my Experience with Psychic Phenomena* by James Albert Pike with Diane Kennedy.

Until then, and that was after more than 50 years of my life, I had not been able to believe in God. I had had many questions over all those years which had bothered and upset me in certain circumstances. But I could never find an answer.

"Why didn't God stop wars?"
"Why did little children have to die?"
"Why were so many people starving and God did not help them."
"Why were so many people so poor, while others were so enormously rich?"
"What was the justice in all this?"
"Why did so many people have to suffer such dreadful diseases?"

Nobody around me could answer these questions. They may have told me that this was just life, the way it is and has always been. I just had to believe in God and not question everything. These things were happening and couldn't be changed.

These answers did not satisfy my curiosity and I refused to believe in a God who allowed wars to happen where so many got killed, or got crippled to lead a miserable life ever after. I saw God as a vengeful entity that punished human beings for their ill deeds. I could believe in a vengeful Deity because of my disgust towards some people and their behaviour: not only towards other people, but especially because of all the cruelty inflicted upon animals all over the world.

There were some people who had told me that God was only

good; that he loved all his children and did not punish them. But they did not elaborate on this.

My doubts were aroused: What a funny way of loving children, by sending them to war to get killed? Would a loving father have his children starving; have them suffering when it could be avoided?

3. The Breakthrough Light Was on its Way

After I had picked up these books with the unusual titles, I started reading and at first couldn't believe what was written. I couldn't stop reading. In every article the Bible was mentioned, so I took my Bible and read the different sections and paragraphs mentioned in the book. It was amazing reading a book, and using the Bible as a reference book right next to it.

The contents were enlightening. Suddenly all my questions were answered. Every section of the book *Soul Search* set one more piece into my lifelong jigsaw puzzle, until the picture was complete: Reincarnation was the answer to it all.

I had found God via reincarnation. For the first time, I could believe why God could not help people, could not stop wars, could not stop the suffering. It was not God punishing people. People punished themselves with their ill deeds, due to the laws of cause and effect; the boomerang effect. What people sow, they will harvest in return. That which they hand out, they will receive.

This was logical to my understanding. A door had opened in my mind to this new way of thinking. It was exciting, and I wanted to know more. The first book on past lives came into focus again and I knew, from then on, this was a subject to be explored in more detail.

4. New Lessons

I was still also listening to the meditation cassettes and needed to upgrade my development on that level. By chance, I found a medium who would give me spiritual lessons once a week. There was also a weekly meditation class I could join, after some introduction to this new field of expertise. This was badly needed, as I was a novice in that field.

In the introduction, this lady told me that I had a soul and a spirit which lived in my body and grounded me to be able to live on earth. She also told me that I had lived before and would live after this life. Living on earth was a school; we were here to learn lessons.

Then she made me write down some affirmations, which I was supposed to say to myself several times a day. I was to look into a mirror as I said them. I followed her advice and had these sentences in my mind all day long:

I love myself. I approve of myself. I accept myself the way I am.

This way of using positive suggestion was new to me. Some of this had been mentioned in the book, though in a different context. Here it was directed at me.

I learned also that I was responsible for everything that I thought, said or did. No one else could be blamed for my own actions.

This got me thinking and I asked myself:
Did I take responsibility for all my actions?
I was an adult. Was I behaving like one?
Did I blame others for my misfortune?

I noticed that I did.

5. Professional Advice

I needed to do this right and sought the help of a psychotherapist. This down-to-earth gentleman, with many fish tanks in his waiting room, set me straight. During our conversations, he pointed out the behaviours of people who had grown up in dysfunctional families, where one blamed the other for this or that. I could follow his examples. It was true: that was the way I had grown up and lived. So many critical remarks, killing enthusiasm immediately, with hardly ever any praise for things done well. Many attempts to dream, or even think in a different direction, had been dismissed as impossible.

The therapist handed me some papers to study, which we would discuss in the next session. I took it all very much to heart. I wanted to learn to become responsible for my thoughts and actions. I wanted to stop blaming others for things that were nobody's fault, but were perhaps just things that happened, or guided lessons from the universe, or God.

It was an eye- and ear-opener, listening to other people on buses or trains, who did exactly the same things as those mentioned in the papers from the therapist: they too blamed others for their troubles. It wasn't only I who hadn't learned to live responsibly. But I wanted to change my behaviour now, quick-smart, as I knew that this behaviour was immature.

This was a very rewarding time, learning so much in so short a time and getting to know about it. But everything had to be put into practice, and that did not happen overnight.

Next time, during my spiritual lessons, I was introduced to proper breathing: not only with my chest, but rather the natural abdominal way we can see in babies. People often forget to inhale deeply during their hectic life styles, and this can cause health difficulties later on. Deep breathing exercises are important during meditation, learning to hold the breath for a few seconds in between. This rhythmic control is very important and has a beneficial, calming effect.

Even though I had learned to relax with a cassette before, now there was no music playing in the background. Now, I heard only the soft voice of the lady teacher, advising me to breathe in deeply, holding for the count of four; stop for a few seconds and then breathe out. Then another count of four, retracting my belly and exhaling every last breath. It is common knowledge that the breath we exhale is inhaled by others.

After I had relaxed completely, the lady guided me into a meditation which relaxed every part of my body. In this way I let go of tensions, and felt refreshed.

Every week there was another exercise to practise with her, but these were also guidelines for me to practise at home. I did not use cassettes. Instead, I meditated with my own guiding thoughts, following the example given in each week's lesson. I made notes in a little booklet I could refer to regularly.

In time, I learned about the Chakras, which I had never heard of before. I learned to use them for self-energy; for healing and finding my colours again. These would include red, blue and purple. It took some time to see orange, green and dark blue; especially to have them 'come on demand,' one after the other. This took many months to achieve.

From our discussions, the lady knew I had some inner problems which needed sorting out. She had scheduled some meditations for these, one after another, for anger, fear, feelings of guilt, forgiveness and self-confidence.

Joining her evening meditation group was always something very special. On arriving at her house, a green light at the front door showed the way to peaceful surroundings, in a cosy living room with couches and dimmed light. There could be 10 to 15 people there, sitting around, waiting for the lady to start the evening session. This she did with a short prayer before guiding us all into meditation. We were given quiet time to explore the task for about 15 minutes. When we were called back, one after the other was asked to tell the group about their experiences.

It was interesting to listen to the others' adventures during their meditation. My efforts had limited in success at the beginning. In time, and with practise, it was more rewarding, and I began to get answers during my mind's explorations. When we had all told our stories, one of us said a final prayer and, with it, we sent out healing messages to people and animals we had heard of who were in distress or in need of healing.

The evening ended with some refreshments around the kitchen table and further happy discussions, rounding off a few very relaxing hours.

Sometimes these meetings included a lecturer on a special subject; some were held on a Saturday and lasted a whole day. We were all interested in learning about Feng Shui, about alternative healing methods for animals, or about the amazing art of reading flowers, which each of us had brought with us. These were delightful occasions in a circle of like-minded men and women, of all ages.

6. Working Out with Meditations

These meditations loosened up my feelings, which had been blocked for so long. I never realised that there was so much anger within me, locked away deep inside. In one meditation, it was as if I was hanging in a balloon that could not land because of all the ballast I kept inside me. There were many labels stuck on to the balloon, which needed to be converted into love. The lesson in this was that the anger had to be realised, then felt and then honestly converted into love. The anger had to be melted away, which was not easy. I needed to do this meditation several times, over a period of time, until I truly noticed these anger feelings had disappeared. Feelings towards people or situations were washed away by feelings of understanding and unconditional love. Then I became aware that my anger really was always directed at myself. I had been angry at myself, and at what I had been doing to myself.

It was similar with fear. The heavy bags, with the labels of the feared subjects hanging onto me, kept me on the bottom of the ocean, unable to keep my head above water. Fear had stifled my emotional response to express myself freely. As with the anger meditation, I had to accept the fear, noticing what it did to me, then release the bags one by one to become lighter and so rise up to the surface. It was such a relief to come out of the cold onto the sunny beach, where a little girl presented me with a gift.

Nothing was learned in one session of meditation... it needed many. These regular exercises helped me to change my attitudes and with it my life. I became a different person. I wondered why it had taken so many years of not knowing, to finally find a way out into the open with this new view of what life was all about. There was so much more to learn, and I was eager to find out.

At one time my teacher gave me a book as a gift. It was Louise L. Hay's *You can heal your life*. I read it and used her affirmations regularly. It has become my constant companion ever since, especially because of "The List" of problems we create for ourselves in our own minds. This was a new way of looking at illnesses, which we create because of dissatisfaction with our surroundings, situations and the people in it.

I learned to use the specific affirmations, which helped me overcome many of my little aches, at the same time as I realised that I was creating and causing them.

It was especially interesting to find out that we are also creating our own pain. Because of my reactions to criticism, I attracted it even more. When we criticise others, we define ourselves.

I read that, because we do not like, nor want to accept a situation, or a trait in a person as it exists, we overlook the possibility of having the same fault in ourselves. We do not recognise it. This is the shadowy side of life that we haven't incorporated into the understanding of ourselves. Criticism brings pain to our inner self. From that time onwards I checked my behaviour and corrected it as quickly as I could.

Pain can be produced in us if we cannot forgive others, or ourselves, for something that happened, maybe years ago. We cling to guilty feelings about a situation, and will not let it go calmly and peacefully. I know of so many people who suffer pain, and wonder whether their pain would go overnight if they could only forgive themselves, and others, for whatever caused the distress.

Sometimes, we do not recognise that we behave in a way that annoys those around us. A very good girlfriend of mine pointed out to me that I often mentioned that I could not afford this or that. I would express my situation as 'poor me', and it did not suit me well. I do not say this any more. There are different ways of saying the same thing; for example 'when the time is right, I'll buy that.'

With all these affirmations it is most important, not only to say them and write them down, we also need to recognise what effect our behaviour is having on ourselves. We are creating a malaise because we are not dealing with our problems in an open and honest way. We need to learn to accept our feelings of hurt; of being ignored; of being criticised; of feeling neglected.

By recognising these 'hurts', we can attempt to deal with our shortcomings and aim to improve ourselves by listening to the opinions of others. If others criticise us for whatever we do; things which are not to their liking, that is their problem, not ours. If we want to be healthy and happy, we cannot constantly change ourselves to the ways others would want us to be. We have to learn that we can only change ourselves. We cannot change other people and their opinion of us.

I have a beautiful little poem a friend once sent me:

"God grant me the serenity to accept the things I cannot change, the courage to change the things I can, and the wisdom to know the difference."

We know we cannot force anyone to love us. If other people cannot accept us the way we are, we have to let them go on their way, so we can be free to be just the way we are. By loving and accepting ourselves, with all our faults, we still deserve to be loved. This knowledge may combat many an ailment, because we have learned to love and approve of ourselves. If we know the reason why we have our off-days, these don't have to make us sick.

That was an important lesson for me to learn at that time, whilst making changes to my life. By trying to be myself, being true to myself, I was taking responsibility for my thoughts, my wants and needs, so as to be able to live a happy, contented and healthy life.

The meditation on guilt brought up all the difficulties I experienced since my parents had emigrated to Australia. This, in years to follow, caused unhappiness, homesickness and illness to my mother. I had blamed myself for asking them to leave their home. My sister and I wanted to be able to care for them in their old age. We had been aware that it is difficult to transplant an old tree and our mother's illness was the result.

The guilt meditation was very difficult. I was sitting, chained to a torture chair in a dungeon. The chains were tying me down from my legs, my arms and body. I could only move a little with my feet, and needed that movement to reach a large pair of pliers with which to cut off labels. The labels had the names of all my guilts, and there were many. It was a great struggle to get to the pliers, get them in to my hands and use them to cut the labels off; to free the chains, one by one. Before cutting the labels off, I had to recognise the guilt and convert it to a better way of dealing with these problems. It was very difficult.

During the meditation, and despite my deep guilt feelings towards my mother's suffering, I had come to realise that my parents had been grown-ups and could have chosen not to come, knowing of the changes they would have to face in a strange country they knew little of.

This was one of the hardest meditations I had to go through. Sometimes, I had to abandon the meditation because of the emotions overwhelming me. It took many attempts to clear up these feelings of having done harm to my parents.

During this time, I had a chance meeting with another medium, who suggested to me that I tune into my feelings, rather than into my thinking mind. Instead of asking myself *"How do I think"*, before making any new decision, his advice was to ask myself *"How do I feel"*. He explained to me that the feelings were the wishes of the soul, to achieve on her life path what she could, for the purpose for which she had incarnated.

It had happened to me many times, when making a decision, that I felt uneasy and uncomfortable about it afterwards. My gut feelings had made me feel ill on occasions. This had been a warning that the decision taken was not the right one. Therefore, I had postponed making any decision before sleeping on it, or taking time out, to be sure that these gut feelings wouldn't be prejudicial.

I followed his advice, and had a few more affirmations to imprint into my mind and thought patterns. Despite all the affirmations I had worked on, my subconscious mind had not fully accepted what I suddenly wanted it to think. It is one thing to desire change, another to get a connection. But the hardest thing of all is to suddenly turn old habits into successful new actions.

There were still many blockages from occurrences in the past that had made me cover my soft spots with a big protective shield. I was aware of it; how easily I reacted to certain people, even those who might have meant well. They could still hurt my feelings with their jocular remarks about my behaviour.

It is hard sometimes not to react to what other people perceive, and to give an honest account of others' vulnerability. Making a joke about another person is often a form of criticism, cloaked with sugar coating. It might be funny for the bystanders, but not necessarily for the subject, or victim.

The meditation on forgiveness was interesting; like climbing down a mine shaft to cut out crystals. I collected many beautiful crystals, each different in colour and size. After I had brought them up to the surface and placed them around me, there were many people close by whom I had hurt during my life. My task was to ask these people, one by one, to forgive me, and offer them a crystal of a size that was appropriate for the hurt I had caused. I remembered them very well, but I could not see them in my mind's eye. It needed many repeat meditations until I could 'see' whether they smiled and forgave me, or not.

Ever since that time, I have tried to apologise to people by mail, in person, or with flowers. Many responded kindly; some ignored my attempt.

The meditation did not end there, because I, too, had been hurt and this meditation extended to those I had to forgive for their behaviour. After that, I had to forgive myself for reacting to these hurts, put them all into a balloon and send them off to heaven with love.

Forgiving oneself is not easy. It takes time to realise that God has forgiven us immediately, whilst we often harbour grudges and hurts for far too long. These can cause malaise. Forgiving means letting go of the grief caused by others, because we have taken it in as pain.

The person who caused the pain may not even know that she or he has hurt us. It is we who are reacting to something that was said or done. Forgiving oneself for being too sensitive towards foolish remarks; or for having done something wrong in a certain situation is, after all, a life experience. We learn from that experience.

Feeling situations means opening up to vulnerability and pain. I never had any problems in feeling the pain of animals that suffer at the hands of human beings, whether on farms, in institutions, or by governments. I was appalled always by the behaviour of the human race in this regard; protested against it; tried to help to solve it. Finally, I gave up, because there is no way in our world ever to change human behaviour. Especially not by me, alone. I did and still do help a few fortunate creatures to have a better life. Others need to rely on the help of the Creator to take them home when ill-treatment on Earth becomes unbearable.

As I am human myself, I had to learn to love unconditionally the human beings around me. We are all as one, after all. What hurts one will also hurt another. It would be incomprehensible to reject human company just for the sake of some people who behave badly. It is a task of a lifetime to understand people, their motives and their often impossible behaviour. Even the most difficult people might better themselves one day, if they have the insight to do so. I often have to remind myself of this, and remember that we are all one—my neighbour breathes in the air I exhale, and vice versa. So does every living creature, great and small. We are all connected by the great force of the universe.

There are advantages in intellectualising one's feelings. Life is much easier that way. But feelings come from the heart and cannot be felt by 'thinking'. With our hearts we connect to our inner being; we empathise with people and with animals and we 'feel' compassion towards others' needs.

It is not necessary to wear ourselves out completely in order to help others. We still have to remember that our first love must be to ourselves. We cannot give love from an empty well. All love overflowing from this well can be used to give away freely, if we continuously replenish the love in our hearts towards ourselves. Feeling and giving belong together.

The meditation on confidence helped me to learn to praise. Praise did not stand high on the agenda during my upbringing, or afterwards. I really needed to learn to give praise to others if I felt it honestly. I never liked flattery and didn't want to mimic that.

During my meditation, I met with an old man who had given me a seed to take good care of. I needed to plant it in the most suitable spot, remove the weeds of negativity, fertilise it with knowledge, water it with patience and continue to nourish it with care. The plant needed a pole of wisdom as support, a shade from wind and sun and a break of inner peace and serenity. After the plant had flowered under the good care it needed, it produced seeds I could harvest, put into a bag and pass on to others.

This was a lovely meditation, which I really enjoyed. It helped me to have confidence in praising a complete stranger, about their looks, or the beautiful clothes they wore. It made me happy when they thanked me with an engaging smile. Sometimes, a small compliment can help a stressed mother in a shop, or a sales lady who is overburdened, or annoyed by others. It is so easy to spread a little love around, and it takes no more than a kind word and a smile.

After my mother had passed on, my father moved further away to be with friends and was cared for there. It was no longer necessary for me to come to town. Additionally, my overnight accommodation was lost.

The opportunities to join groups at night became fewer. I stayed at home in the bush with my work on the land; with the joy of animals and grandchildren often to join me. It was a peaceful time, with hard work, but I did not mind that.

Visitors came and told me of their spiritual adventures. One friend gave me a gift of meditation cassettes, two of which included guided meditations to past life regressions by Denise Linn.

Despite living far out in the sticks, I occasionally attended workshops or lectures in the neighbouring bigger town. Subjects like Astrology, from the Inner Peace Movement, or for the purpose of learning remedial massage. Some friends gave me a place to stay overnight. These outings were enjoyable and benefited, not only me, but later on friends and family, on whom I practised my new-found expertise.

The opportunity presented to learn the art of laying-on-of-hands, Reiki. The tutor came to my home to teach the students I had gathered.

This was another step, and very rewarding in helping myself and others. I used to include some Reiki in my massage treatment for clients. It astonished me and my friends how well we could create this healing warmth via our hands on others' body parts. I often use Reiki on my animals, although this art of healing is not widely known, especially in the country. My massage lady was rejected at one venue, where she and her husband used to massage people. Suddenly, the hall had been emptied because a rumour had spread that they used 'black magic'. They had to stop using the Reiki energy before their clients would return. Ignorance still remains.

In the meantime, I continued reading dozens of books on spiritual matters, on Astrology and Reincarnation, to improve my knowledge. Reading about these subjects was like a drug to which I seemed to be addicted. The questions they brought up seemed to be inexhaustible.

My daily meditations still helped me to relax and calm my mind; improving my inner explorations with advice derived from cassettes. Now and then, I tried the cassettes on past life regressions, but always finished feeling drained by emotions, and in tears. I did not know why, because I did not see anything, only felt a deep hurt. It took half a year until I could distinguish something; my first pictures of certain events that had happened to me in a past life.

During this time of learning and the widening of my mental horizons, I realised that there weren't many people around me with whom I could discuss these subjects. Some people were interested in Astrology, and would have liked me to enlighten them on their chart. But I did not want to give Astrology readings as I was not experienced enough. As soon as I started talking about my other interests—spiritual matters, meditation and reincarnation—people looked at me in astonishment, doubting whether or not I was right in my mind. It was strange to me that no one wanted to even hear what I had to say about the subject. Their discussions concentrated on their daily routines: the weather, politics, sports or their illnesses. I withdrew from these conversations and kept my distance.

It did not greatly bother me to have very few friends with like-minded interests. Work, books and studies kept me busy. All was well in my life—as Louise L. Hay would say.

I did wonder, though, why I had suddenly been awakened to these new insights, while others around me had not. I had been ignorant of these facts of what life is all about for far too long, and others still were. Soon, I became aware that I was powerless to convince any of these people about my newest way of thinking, because they were as stubborn and unwilling to see my way as I had been, when a kind friend had tried to convince me to believe in God and change my mind. These people weren't ready to understand.

A little door in my mind had opened. Suddenly, I knew how lucky I was, to have been touched by God's Grace.

Even though my first questions had been answered, new questions came to mind all the time:

"Why hadn't I learnt these very simple tasks when I was a child?"

"Wouldn't my life have changed if I had learned to take responsibility for my thoughts and actions earlier in life?"

"If I had known during my younger days that I could not blame anyone else for my thoughts and ill-deeds, I wouldn't have had to face them coming back to me via cause and effect. Why wasn't I told?"

For more than 50 years, I had been wandering in a wilderness of not knowing the facts of life; of having struggled, despaired and, only through good fortune, achieved an arrival at this point in my life.

My spiritual teacher had enlightened me that I had a guardian angel with me all the time, and I came to realise that it must have been this guardian angel who helped me along on the most difficult stretches of my life's path. My problems had mainly been emotional, as I have been well able to handle the physical side of living. I was strong, but emotions could easily knock me over. I had lost my nerve, and the way forward, on occasion. This new way of thinking settled me down towards a positive outlook. Here I am, believing in God and in another life after life. There is no way back now. I am a believer.

Only now I can answer my latest questions. There had been so many important lessons for me to learn first. These were necessary for my character-building. All these ups and downs had been needed to earn a certain level of accomplishment. I was granted the ability to see colours from my third eye. These colours had a big impact on me. After I had found the book and read it, together with references to the Bible, my mind's door was opened up to the wisdom I received. Suddenly, I could understand and take it in. I was ready and on my way. I am forever grateful for these wonderful events.

7. Some of My Past Life Experiences

Occasionally, I travelled to the neighbouring town for appointments and shopping. I took the chance of meeting up with my spiritual teacher for another lesson in meditation. These had different outlooks for positive thinking, for de-cluttering the mind, letting go of unneeded luggage or emotional baggage. My tutor also tried past life regressions with me, but they did not provide any insight for me.

I continued my past life regressions at home and finally, one day, I felt I could see what was going on. During the journey through the tunnel I felt that my body had changed. When I stepped out into that past life, I saw myself as a young girl with long blond hair; a child of about ten years in a long white dress. I was barefooted and was walking in front of some priests towards the top of a hill to be sacrificed.

This was the reason why I had been crying in earlier meditations. Now I could feel, in this small and fragile girl's body, the despair of not being able to run away. The fear of what was going to happen to her made her shiver. However, her pride tried to control that fear. She had been born and reared by high-ranking parents. She needed to be brave for them. She walked proud and upright towards the scaffold on that hill, overlooking a beautiful valley, where she had to kneel down. Her eyes were covered and her hair bound to one side. The executioner came with his axe and executed her.

The church leaders wore white tunics and high hoods, like priests in the Catholic church. However I could neither distinguish the religion, nor the country.

This was my first experience of this kind. The emotional shock of it all overwhelming me completely. I was in tears and, even though I heard the voice of the cassette: *"Let your body go... You are not dead... You are floating... Go to the light,"* I could neither follow it nor forgive any one in that past life. I was shaken. I needed time to get over it.

This meditation explained to me why I was reluctant to join church services; especially why I loathed seeing those church festivals aimed at encouraging thousands of people to join mass rallies. I could never respect those hooded and fancy-clothed church leaders for their masquerade.

After a while, I meditated again and found out about the following life:

I was a middle-aged, tall man with blond, scruffy hair, clad in pants and a white, open, long-sleeved shirt with boots, standing on top of a hill overlooking the valley that I loved so much. I was Irish, angry and frustrated, cursing and crying out loud, because circumstances were forcing us all to leave our home. I did not want to leave. All my neighbours and their families, including my own, were ready, packed and leaving for foreign lands. I could not make up my mind. It was heartbreaking to feel his frustration and pain. Finally, I gave in and followed my people. My wife turned around and was pleased to see me.

I saw a long track of people, young and old; many children of all ages amongst them, carrying burdensome luggage; some driving carts; all walking on a sandy road and disappearing into the distance afar.

I found out no more. However, this migration of Irish people to foreign lands seemed to have been forced on them by the potato blight famine.

I was surprised though, that I had been a man in that past life, an Irish man. No wonder I liked the Irish dancers so much. My travels never took me to Ireland, but I saw documentaries from that beautiful country with the harsh climate.

On another occasion I found myself on the Mountain in Peru, the mysterious Machu Picchu. I was a young girl, a teenager, who had been brought up to this mountain top, together with other girls. Religious leaders of our tribe had selected us from our families to be sacrificed to the gods that had brought hardship upon the tribe. Our deaths would make peace with the gods who had deserted the tribe. After a ceremony, we were pushed from the mountain top into a deep pool of water, down below, to drown. I felt the agony of being in the water, of not being able to hold on to anything on the steep and slippery sides of this water-storage pond. We screamed and pleaded to be rescued, but to no avail. When our strength left us and we were unable to hold our head above the water level, we sank and drowned.

As a school girl I had been interested in the ancient history of South America; the Incas, the Mayan people. Having read a book on the archaeological finds, and other features, I watched films and documentaries and always wished to be able to travel to Peru. Once I enquired at a travel agency, but I did not have sufficient funds. I asked the Organiser of this trip to buy a poncho for me. She did so and posted it to me. It is still in my wardrobe. This past life reminded me of a life there at another time. How amazing are our memory banks.

The fear of drowning, or jumping into deep water, showed up when I had swimming lessons at a Club, as a teenager. I liked swimming, then, and still do today; but I never liked jumping from a board. When it became necessary, during that course, for me to jump from a one-metre board into the pool, that was fine. However, jumping from a three-metre board made me very anxious afterwards. I refused any further jumps and left the Swimming Club and training course. One of my school-friends enjoyed jumping from a ten-metre platform with great delight. She could not get enough of it. I've never attempted another jump from on high.

The next meditation took me to North America. I was a young American-Indian squaw, with long black hair, which was kept tight and together with a headband around my forehead. I was running, in fright, because enemies on horses were pursuing me. These riders, from another tribe, rode faster than my feet could take me. Soon, they came close enough to fire an arrow, which struck me in the neck, killing me instantly. I fell forward on my face into the sand.

At that time, I followed the instructions and forgave all who hurt and killed me. This changed something within my neck, which had been a bother after my head-on car collisions and resulting whiplash. The difficulties diminished. Was it my willingness to forgive? I believe it was.

In the following meditation I turned out to be Russian; a very old man with long grey beard and hair to match. I was very ill, resting on a Russian oven bench because it was so very cold in this simple cottage... and it was winter.

I had my family around me. My three grandchildren were very close to me. I loved them so much. I was dying, but I did not want to die.

I did not want to leave my grandchildren. I wanted to postpone leaving them alone. They were still so young.

I felt this old man's pain and sorrow at leaving his small grandchildren, as there didn't seem to be enough security and protection for them without his being around.

Unfortunately, I could not find out more about his past life. The home was poorly constructed and he seemed to have been the only man left in this family to work and care for these dependents.

I found school history lessons about Russia exciting. Stories about the Tsar; of the beautiful country with its animals; its vast distances. I learned about Siberia; about the lives of the many peasants; of those who were cruelly-treated and unpaid. These were the workforce of royalty and the rich of that land, prior to the communist revolution. Books and films, men's choirs and dancers are known world-wide and are famous for their artistic performances. I read about the ballerina Anna Pavlova, who was an illustrious dancer, my star when I was a young girl.

At that stage I knew that there was a reason to remember life in that country.

On another occasion, I was a maid or a governess for a small boy, whom I dearly loved. The house where the family that employed me were living was near the pylons of a Harbour Bridge, possibly in England. This looked similar to the Sydney Harbour Bridge, but was not that. It was a large house. The people I was working for were very wealthy. The entrance hall of that house was large, with black and white terracotta tiles on the floor. There were large side windows, some green plants placed around and the hall was sparsely furnished. I wore women's boots with laces, a long dress or skirt and blouse closed around the neck. The boy wore a cap, knickerbockers and high boots as well. We went for walks.

One day the family left and I had to stay behind. I missed the young lad; it was a sad occasion.

I followed the instructions on the cassette. I saw myself as an old maid with grey hair, sitting alone in a chair, looking out of the window where

I passed away.

These regression cassettes always tell you to go on, in order to find out what happens at the end of that life. It is always soothing, though, to listen to the advice. We haven't died, only our body has, while our spirit is alive and floating towards the Spirit Realm.

It became easier to use the regression cassettes. The questions I wanted answers to, before I went into the tunnel, were always connected to problems I encountered at that time. I sometimes wondered about my most recent insights, most of which I never anticipated.

In the following meditation I was again a woman; this time an Aboriginal woman. I lived with my tribe in a camp where we gathered bush tucker. The time was after the invasion of the British into Australia. We had to be careful, as we were often chased by settlers. We had to hide and were terrified. We wore few clothes.

This meditation gave me an answer as to why I migrated to Australia.

I liked my new country from the beginning and could cope with the challenges it presented. For the most part it was the language. At the outset, speaking it was a problem. I have always felt empathy towards Aborigines. I learned about their culture through books—especially those written by Mary Gilmore. Some of the stories saddened me to tears. I always felt deeply about the cruelty inflicted on the true Australians and the way they had been treated. I never could watch films about the settlers and the red-coat British soldiers who pursued the natives. I avoided watching documentaries on the subject. It upset me; I could feel the injustice. This meditation and other similar ones gave me an answer.

In a past-life regression in June 1999, I was again an Aboriginal woman, who was kept prisoner at a camp for English soldiers. This was in 1790. I had to cook, wash and clean for these soldiers. Other Aboriginal men were held there with chains on their feet and arms. We were all silently resistant and looking for opportunities to escape. One day, this opportunity arose and I was able to help the men with implements I found to cut their chains. Then we escaped. When I was old, I lived with my tribe and was free. We were all sitting around a fire in the desert somewhere. I died there.

In a past-life regression in July 1999, I was a young Aboriginal boy living with my tribe. My son-in-law, Bill, was my father and he was teaching me to hunt and fish. We were sitting around the camp fire and the women were preparing certain foods. I recognised many of my son-in-law's friends and relatives; we were all there together. This time was prior to the settlement of Australia. I fell off a cliff and died young.

My son-in-law and I had our problems in understanding each other. However in time we came to a silent, but mutual understanding.

I sometimes wondered why he was always so protective of me. He was always there when I needed help. When I told him about this past life where he had been my father, he did not believe it. He still likes to sit around a fire with friends in the bush and likes to fish, though hunting is out. It is of no importance to me whether people believe this or not. Suffice to say that it explains and answers my questions.

8. Living in the Bush

While living by myself on a 25-acre property, 10 km from the nearest town, I felt isolated from others, as I did not have a car. My daughter lived nearby, so help was available if I needed it.

There must have been a reason why, during my whole life, I always ended up living away from towns, or transport. This was explained to me whilst attending a lecture at the Inner Peace Movement. In a former life, in the 12th century, I had annoyed my then husband by leaving him. He put a curse on me such that I would always find myself isolated somewhere, away from opportunities. Considering this curse, I could relate to it. However, events and happenings had often come to me when I could not catch them outside my home.

Being single and living alone never bothered me. I had enough company from friends visiting me, because I lived in such a beautiful area. My grandchildren were growing up and I enjoyed seeing them often. Children are so honest in their appreciation and they still have a connection to the Spirit World. One day, my smallest grandson told me that my father was visiting and sitting in his armchair in my living room with us. I could not see him, but he surely recognised his Opa, even though my father had passed on whilst my grandson was still a toddler.

The children were open-minded and enjoyed the meditation cassette for children I had bought for them. We also used crystals and I explained to them how to use them. I showed them also the laying-on-of-hands in case of injuries. However, when adults around them do not continue to instruct children, they will forget easily. Too many new things come into their lives in their early years. As soon as school starts, children usually lose their contact with the universe, as strict rules and disciplines direct them away from it. I enjoyed the times I had with them whilst it lasted.

That people are at one with all other creatures in the universe became clear to me whilst studying the animals around me. Different kinds of wildlife visited my place, such as kangaroos, wallabies, possums, bandicoots and birds of all kinds, as well as my own domesticated ones. As I used to feed the wallabies, wild wood ducks would occasionally come to the feeding lot. Once, my place became a meeting place for all the wood ducks in the area. There were more than a hundred flying in and noisily talking to each other. They had not come to feed. They must have felt safe at my place because I was watching them close-by.

All wild animals get to know people living in their territory, and I was living in theirs. People forget that we are intruding upon their usual run, where they feed regularly. When we put up fences, we are making it difficult for wildlife. They injure themselves, or are locked out completely from their grazing areas. Territorial fights occur when these locked-out animals have to use other areas for grazing. Areas where they don't belong, or are not wanted by animals which frequent neighbouring areas.

My property was fenced, but this was no hindrance to the wildlife which came to graze there. They drank from my dam or the water containers I put out for them, or would rest under bushes, even very close to my verandah, for hours.

Whilst watching the animals' behaviour, I noted that humans are just another animal. We are so similar in our behaviour, though with some exceptions. Animals fight or argue over food, fight for mates, reject others' offspring, reject older and sick animals. They can be very cruel this way, because such animals usually lack the strength to get the feed they need to survive. There is no charity in the animal world, and this behaviour is a death sentence to most. Animals seem to have a very close connection to the Spirit World, as they give up when they are unable to fight for survival. They lay down when ill or injured; wasting away until their Spirit is taken within a few days. Animals suffer in silence, but their wounds hurt as much as ours. Many people believe that animals have no feelings. How wrong they are.

Animals get hungry and eat what they need during the day or night, but they are never greedy, nor do they hoard food they do not need. That's where we break the rules: humans are greedy; are never satisfied and are often quite wasteful.

I like animals, even snakes and spiders; in some ways, I love them more than people. They are honest in their behaviour. They may scratch you, if you hurt them. However, if you respect and love them, they will usually love you, too, and you can rely on their friendship. One never knows with human beings...

The older I became, noticing the little things around me became my main way of looking at life. Nature and wildlife gave me a certain peace and understanding. My eyes and feelings did not want to accept, at first, that one animal eats the other. Some young birds were thrown out of the nest by their parents, because a cuckoo had laid one of its eggs in their nest.

The nest was too small to provide room for all its inhabitants. The larger fledgling was very demanding and forced the death of the rest of the brood.

This is only one example of behaviour that is comparable to that of humans. Human cuckoos do much more harm when they invade neighbouring countries, killing and destroying. Human behaviour is always more brutal and destructive. Birds see to it that the fittest of their brood survive. Human cuckoos are only after money and power, and consider only themselves.

There is so much beauty in nature. Insects work hard to fulfil their life's aim in the short time they have. Some only have a few days; others, like the honey bee, a few weeks. She lives six weeks, and makes long trips to collect heavy loads of honey or pollen on her legs to bring home to her hive. In her short life, she collects about a half a teaspoonful of honey. I learned to respect these creatures of nature. They are clearly the product of a master builder. Their tiny bodies are built to perfection, including a brain that knows exactly what to do, and what life is all about for them, to perform the job they have to do.

Insects are highly underrated by humans, who have done so much harm with insecticides, destroying the balance in nature, with the result that more and more poison is needed to grow food for humans. People have so much residue of all the poisons in their bodies, it is no wonder that so many suffer from illnesses caused by just living, eating and breathing in our polluted environment.

It would be a benefit to all of us if we learned to respect our environment, and all the animals in it, as the survival of our own species depends on it. Man is arrogant and ignorant of the most important facts: Humans need all the insects and the animals in their natural habitats for their own survival.

As I have learned, I can only hope that others will mend their ways for a better understanding.

9. More Past Life Regressions

During this time I was involved with a friend who was married. His wife was not well, and they lived apart in different houses and towns. The man lived near my place. The following regression changed our friendship:

It was my wedding day. It was sunny, and the wedding was held in a large beautiful garden of my parents' big white house, with wide terraces around and servants. I think it was in Ireland. I wore a bridal outfit and looked beautiful. The bridegroom (who was my friend in this life) was tall, slim and handsome. We danced and laughed and played with the guests, but there was a girl to whom the bridegroom was very attracted (his wife in this life). He always included her, attended to her, neglecting me. This made me very unhappy.

Later on, we lived on a farm. My husband and I worked very hard. I bore him three children and was carrying the infant on my arm, bringing him lunch onto the field where he ploughed the soil.

In the end, I was laying in our brown wooden marriage bed, dying after a new baby in childbirth. My husband had kept contact with his girlfriend during all our marriage and, while I was sick in bed, she was already taking over my household duties. I felt betrayed but just could not help my situation.

This had been the second time that I saw clearly the faces of the people I knew in a past life. Our love triangle had to change. I told my friend and suggested to him that it would be best for him to stick to his promise to his wife, this time around, as he did not keep his promise to me in that past life. We still stayed friends, though differently. He had an understanding of my spiritual adventures and could believe what I had discovered.

10. Insights into Past Lives' lessons

Through my past-life regressions, I found out that I had been a different sex in some of my lives, and could be either a woman or a man. I also noticed that, even though I was often reborn into the same large group of people, we were not in the same family structures. The connections were different, and this was sometimes confusing.

I'm sure this is not just happening in my life, but is a common theme. Our children from past lives can return as lovers in this life, and vice versa. Passion can be such a strong force, breaking down all barriers of common sense. We often meet people we feel we know so well; to whom we are subconsciously connected from a past life. This can result in confused relationships in this life, and be the cause of adultery, marriage break-ups and even incest.

As well, my past lives as an Aboriginal, a Native American and as an Indian person in India showed me that we also change the colour of our skin, race and religion.

I discovered that I used to live in many different countries, even continents. This would not agree with a genealogical search, because my soul was not restricted to my family tree alone. It resided in different realms, widely separated throughout the world.

I made a practice of reading through many books in order to discover more detailed descriptions of others' past life experiences. Books from the Association for Research and Enlightenment, Edgar Cayce's A.R.E., offered a valued resource. These books give thorough accounts derived from Edgar Cayce's life readings and answered many of my questions.

According to my A.R.E. readings, we change sexes in order to feel the pain that we have caused others. Males need to learn how life feels in a woman's body; they need to learn of the burden many women carry or take on for the sake of the family. Females have to learn how difficult it can be to be a provider for a family in a man's world.

We change races for the same reason, in order to experience life from the point of view of those of other creeds and cultures.

It seems to me that, through our past lives, we get an opportunity to restore lost favour, especially if we have been cruel and abusive to others, such as children, the elderly, people of a different race or religion, handicapped or disabled people, and animals.

No person is born innocent; no one has a clean slate. Every baby has had past lives and becomes reincarnated with the aim of improving on its Karma. Children who die young may have chosen to live only through this one experience; to learn from it and teach compassion to the people around them. For others who die young, perhaps there were only a few lessons in this life.

Even the choice of parents depends on our behaviour in former lives. Did we behave lovingly and in a caring way towards our children in those lives? If we did not, we cannot expect to be born into a loving, caring family in this life. Depending on other effects, we may have to live with parents who behave exactly as we behaved towards our children. If we abused, mistreated, or offered very little comfort to our own children, how can we expect loving parents in this life?

Children learn so much from the behaviour of parents, their siblings and family members around them; lessons they just pick up while growing up. After all, it is in the family where children learn to compete for attention, for love; learn about aggression, jealousy, envy, hatred and malice. We learn, while young, how to handle and deal with these issues. Later, we can choose which of the characteristics we want to adopt to for ourselves and leave behind those we do not agree with.

We each create our lives through our own thoughts and deeds. Due to the universal law of cause and effect, we receive that which we have earned: as we sow, so shall we reap. If we do not give love in all honesty to others, we cannot hope to receive love in return. The love or help we give to one person may not necessarily return to us from the same source, but a loving, caring and compassionate person will always receive loving returns, whether it be as good health, helpful friends or special circumstances.

The Bible says that God will provide for all our needs, but many people feel the need to help others. I have met people who live for the good of others and for animals; people seem to be selflessly involved in doing good in the world, forgetting themselves. But what happens to our own strength if we do not care well enough for ourselves?

There is a fairy tale by the Brothers Grimm, *Star Talers (Sterntaler)*, where a poor orphaned girl gives away her last singlet to the needy. The reward of many golden coins comes falling down from heaven into her lap. Every little thought or help, given freely, will also benefit the giver.

Sometimes, though, we can cause ourselves to become ill, when people or situations make us uncomfortable. Even a minor incident or misunderstanding can cause resentment. If we do not let it go quickly and forgive, resentment can fester. There are no coincidences in life. We can bring on our own misfortune with a hasty word or a wilful act.

Cause and effect means:
If we love, we will receive love in abundance in return.
If we hate; others will hate us.
If we steal; others will steal from us.
If we hurt someone; others will hurt us.
If we murder; somebody will murder us.
It is not God punishing us; we are punishing ourselves.

It seems to me that no one can cast the first stone at another, because no one knows what we have been or done in former lives. We might have been the good, the bad, or the ugly; the torments, the crooks, or thieves; some may even have murdered. We have all been in wars where horrendous deeds are perpetrated on others: torture, rape, murder, burning houses, destroying other people's lives. We never know when our Karma will catch up with us.

I remember well, hearing as a little girl that there was no hiding from God. God sees everything. In a way it is so. If not through God personally, then through cause and effect: the universe records our every little thought and deed and returns it to us in kind.

Subconsciously, we know about fear and pain, but we never seem to learn from this knowledge. Human beings are a warring race, and have never learnt to live in peace for long. Looking at the world around me, I know for certain that peace on earth will never prevail. Peace on earth is something we can only find within ourselves, through meditation and in solitude.

We need to learn to be good if we want to have a good life, but life often gets in the way of good intentions. We want to enjoy ourselves, especially while we are young, and it is necessary to experience life in order to learn. So we meet the challenges and live life as it is dealt out to us. The person who never tries anything will not do anything wrong, but will also not learn anything new.

No one knows when and how we will die. We all have just this moment and we may as well enjoy it, because it never returns. When I woke up to this life truth, I considered it as the only true justice on earth.

11. Past Life Regressions, continued

I continued with meditations and sometimes found myself in a past life that surprised me.

One day I had changed into a young Indian boy who wore silk clothes, shoes made of cloth and a turban. I lived in a palace in elegant surroundings. I was very distinguished, well cared for. However I was very lonely. No body belonged to me. I was looking for company as I walked through the rooms of the palace. I could not see any servants. The place was deserted. I walked on outside through the garden and over empty spaces beyond, far from the palace. No one was looking for me and I could find no one. I walked on; it was a desolate place where the bushes were dried up by the hot sun. I was lost when it got dark. I could not find my way back. I ended up in a desert with sand dunes. I was not able to fend for myself in this harsh environment. I died of dehydration.

This young boy wore jewellery and very costly clothes. However, something must have happened such that the servants disappeared and left him behind. I could not find out more. I felt the sadness; the despair. It seemed as if he was the only person wandering through that large area of land.

I was never attracted towards travelling to India, because of the overcrowding in that land. Documentaries pictured the country as beautiful, with people in traditional dress. These are very colourful, indeed. The poverty of most of its inhabitants, however, is appalling to me. The structure of their religions seems foreign and strange to me, especially the cruelty towards the group called "Untouchables".

The traditional values of India are mainly for the benefit of men and the rich, who can treat women the way they see fit, and the law permits. Any country whose religion places women's worth lower than a sheep's will never rate as free and democratic to me. This country is best looked at from afar, despite the high culture, the artistry of buildings and the wonderful poetry written with their music and dances.

When I was young, I liked some films which portrayed the 'then' India in *The Elephant Boy*, and a German film *Der Tiger von Ashnapur*. This featured a dancer called La Yana. It is remarkable that some Yogis like Paramahanse Yogananda have such a great following of believers in their disciplines. Still, the asceticism of this cult has not changed India for the better, concerning the poor and their caste system, their laws and traditions.

When migrating to Australia via British Airways, the airplane landed in Bombay. We could see all those street people camping, living in shacks along the runway. It was shocking that hundreds, if not thousands of people had to live under those derelict shelters. It was not really an advertisement designed to present India to travellers.

Going back into the past, I saw myself as a young woman, wearing a traditional dress (Dirndl) of the Swiss Alps, with a dark red skirt and a white blouse. I was a farm girl (Bauernmädchen) in Switzerland. I arrived with my bundle of belongings to work on the farm in a Swiss pub (Gaststätte). There were tables outside that I had to wait on when guests visited. This Swiss chalet was located in the high mountains. I also worked in the fields of this farm. Moving forward, I married and had several children. I died among family members.

The time given was 1829.

Actually, I have never visited Switzerland in this life, and I wondered whether these high mountains had been in Austria, a holiday destination my husband and I visited several times. I like mountains, always did; even though it frightened me driving along serpentine roads through the Alps. It is a wonderful feeling, though, to stand on top of a mountain and look around: a feeling of achievement after the strenuous climb. I ascended a few lower mountains in Bavaria and Austria.

Some of my favourite pictures are of mountains, of flowers and chalets.

They are hanging on my walls.

In another excursion into my past lives, I was a boy at school, aged about 10 or 12 years, with long, blond hair and wearing a brown uniform with knickerbockers and high black-leather boots.

I was playing, arguing and wrestling with other boys in the school ground. There was a sandy field around a red brick school. There were large trees in the yard. The teacher was my daughter in this life—or was she my mother? She was a tall woman, dressed in a long brown costume and a white blouse with buttons high up on the neck. She was wearing high booties, as was the custom during those times, and a hat. The schoolmaster was my son-in-law of this life—or was he my father then? He wore a black outfit with white shirt and hat. His figure was stout and he was elderly.

I was still a young lad when I died, in a cornfield. I was wearing an open shirt with ragged pants. I had long hair, was barefoot and working with a fork. There was an accident involving a horse. I could not see clearly how. Hay was brought in with the help of horse and wagon.

I could not find out the time or the country. It was in the west, I assume North America, and we were white people.

I wonder whether there is a connection, as my son-in-law never was keen on my daughter's riding ambitions. After years of riding her horse, and enjoying it, she eventually gave up because she always heard from him that it was a dangerous sport.

Another experience, in a past life regression, was when I turned out to be a young woman with black hair in a simple traditional dress, dancing on a sandy beach. I was waiting for something or someone to turn up, always looking out to sea. No one came for me. Other people appeared. They were seafaring men, busy with their boats and nets, preparing to go out to sea.

When I was old and wearing a long black frock with black boots, I was walking along the beach again, looking into the distance, waiting for something or someone that did not come.

This insight was sad and depressing. I could feel the loneliness of this woman. She was waiting for loved ones to come home.

A year after that, I found myself as a cloaked person. At first I thought I was a man, but it turned out I was a nun or a nurse in a very dark, miserable hospital. There were many injured and dying people in the big hall of a building, like a castle. This hall seemed to be located in a cellar, somewhere, during a war. There were many women dressed like me and we were helping the sufferers. For some, it was a hopeless situation. We all tried to relieve some of the pain and cleaned away the dirt, day and night. It was exhausting for all the nurses and doctors, though there were only a few doctors around. The males were medical orderlies. We women tried what we could to provide comfort for these sick people in our care.

Later on, I was living as an old woman in a home where I felt loved. I went to the light, forgave all and died.

There were some brief experiences. Once, I was a young man in a green outfit with a hat, carrying a bow and arrow, and with a small bundle of possessions. I was a rebel, living in the woods, fighting with others against injustices brought on by Authorities.

When dying, I was surrounded by friends and had made peace with myself and the world around me.

I always liked the idea of Robin Hood and the mythology about this prominent figure in films and stories. I could always understand the notion of fighting for justice in a world that is lacking support for the disadvantaged.

In another life, I was a blond-haired young woman in traditional dress in Germany, living in a large farm house in the year 1645. The farmhouse looked like the one I lived in as a tenant, with my mother and sister, as a young girl during World War II.

I could not explore this any further, because I fell asleep. On my regression tapes, it says, in the introduction, that we may only find out something that is helpful for this life. This meditation showed me, though, that we had met these people on the farm in a life before.

When we arrived at the farmstead (Bauernhaus) in 1944, we were complete strangers to this family. We were forced on them by the Government, because we were evacuees. They took us in like family members, and looked after the two of us children for nine weeks. My mother had to go to hospital the next day. The two years we knew these people, and the township we lived in, I still remember and cherish as some of the best years of my childhood. I learned everything there about farm life that I would put it into practise many years later.

In the following past life regression, I was a tall stately farmer in breeches, boots and suspenders. I was living alone on a farm, working very hard, ploughing the field with my horse.

Even though I was prepared, by now, to reveal unusual happenings, I wondered why I was crying all the time during one of my next meditations. It was foggy, and I did not know and could not see where I was. I saw a bricked-in doorway as part of an ancient building. There was a very sad, hopeless feeling within me. Then I could see myself as a nun, in black clothing. I was sad, lonely and still young when I died in that cloister.

I made a follow-up meditation and found out the following:

I was a beautiful young woman with long black hair. I was a parlour maid, and wore a simple cotton dress-apron with a white blouse. I was barefoot. This was a royal household, where I had to curtsy and dress a tall woman (my girlfriend in this life) in a beautiful golden-yellow gown. She stood high on a footstool, because I had to mend and sow something on her gown. I had to look up to her. A tall, good looking young man (my girlfriend's husband in this life), who was either her son or brother, turned up. He liked me and showed kindness towards me. I liked him too. The woman was very powerful and did not like the young man having any contact with me, a lower ranked employee.

I died as a nun in black clothing. I forgave all in that life, even though I could not find out more.

Then I had a dream the following night:

I was in the employ of a high-ranked royal woman in Spain or France. I was the daughter of a low-ranked peasant. I was quite beautiful, with my long black hair. The son of this woman fancied me so much that he made advances towards me. I loved him and fell for him and we had sexual encounters. However, when I fell pregnant, he would not step down to marry me, a commoner. His mother paid my salary and sent me home to my parents, disgraced. My parents handed me over to the Catholic nuns.

In that dream, there was no mention of what happened to my baby. I died sad and broken-hearted as a black-clad nun.

Through a woman who was a medium, I found out two years later that my baby had been a boy. The nuns in that cloister arranged for him to become a priest.

These three meditations gave me answers I needed. These two people turned up in this life and we were good friends, until a certain time when fate caught up with us again. I wonder over how many more lifetimes I have to meet this man on the rebound, and never as a husband. The chemistry between us seems to be very strong whenever and wherever we meet.

In the year 2003, one of my past life regressions shocked me. I was a young French girl then, dressed for battle, riding a horse with many other soldiers, using a sword like those riding with me, fighting a furious battle. We stormed a city and won. We were victorious and deliriously happy about it.

However, moving forward in that life, I was dragged before a court and accused of betrayal. I could not defend myself and was condemned to be burned at the stake. When standing there on the pile of sticks, bound to a wooden pole, I was terrified but also prayed. I did not feel any pain; I was numb and left my body before the flames touched me. I forgave all.

Another meditation showed me a beautiful cave, with stalactites and wonderful formations on the walls. Then I saw the golden face of an old man and no more. Just in case, I forgave all.

A few months later, I was a black-haired, beautiful gypsy girl in a colourful outfit: a half-length, red, wide skirt with a white blouse, half sleeves and a black vest. One could see my slim legs and feet in tiny thin sandals. I was dancing on a cobbled street in a town somewhere, entertaining the public. Later, I also danced with a partner (the husband of my girlfriend in this life) in Spanish dress and costume, to guitar music. I used castanets in my hands to the rhythm of our shoes and the clapping of hands. We drove and travelled in gypsy caravans, enjoyed fiery, hot-tempered lovemaking and lived a wild life where we were not fenced in.

When I was old, I read cards and the hands of passers-by and earned my living from it. I wore a black dress, then, and had many family members around me. However, the man I loved—'my man'—was not around. I felt a longing that hurt.

Eight months later, another meditation:

I was a tall, blond, beautiful, slim-figured woman about 30 years of age. I wore a white tunic with golden sandals, just like the women of Rome used to wear in Caesar's time. I was living in a building that resembled a palace. Seeing myself, I started crying and feeling so unhappy. I was a slave and used for the pleasure of men there. I also had to play the harp, serve food and massage men. I felt deeply resentful of all the things they made me do.

Originally, I came from Northern foreign lands and did not speak the language. My rejection of this way of life, that was forced on me, resulted in punishment for it.

I still felt lonely and homesick for my country of birth, when I was dying, but I had made peace within myself. I could forgive others and myself when I was in the spirit realm. I did not recognise familiar faces but just felt what had been so hurtful to me.

When I studied Latin at University, a fondness for this ancient language developed in me. The stories we had to translate fascinated me. However, the grammar was very complicated and I failed the second course. It needed much more time to study than I could spare.

Shortly after this regression, I undertook a follow-up meditation, because I wanted to know more. The husband of my girlfriend in this life was a Roman soldier of high rank, who had brought me with him as a conquest from the northern areas of Europe. He had placed me in the palace where he lived with his wife. He came to me whenever it pleased him. I loved him, but did not deserve this treatment. It hurt me and I was not free to leave. I was there at his mercy and had to do what he demanded. I finally ran away, either killing myself or being killed in pursuit. During the search for me, he was seen to be bending over my dead body, crying, and being very unhappy.

I forgave him, even though it was hard. I was crying at the end of the meditation.

Some meditations are emotionally draining, because I can feel the pain suffered in that life. If I am able to forgive in the end, it eases the pain still connected to the soul and this can be a release.

In another confrontation with my past, I was a young blond-haired girl of about 16 or 17 years of age, wearing a light summer dress. I was playing in a park-like garden with my girlfriends. Suddenly, a group of men entered the scene. They talked to us at first, but later on forced me away with them. I screamed for help, and fought but could not free myself. One of the men took me away, but I do not know where to or what happened after that. The fright eased, but I did not find out where I ended up or how I died. I was still very young. I could not see the face of the young man who took me. He seemed known to me, but it still was not right that he took me with him by force.

I wonder whether this was the abduction from the northern regions of Europe by Roman soldiers. I never made a follow-up meditation.

A few months later, I turned out to be a child in a meditation. I was barefoot, in rags and terrified. Many of us were herded together, like cattle in a corral, watched over by Roman soldiers. We were prisoners or slaves. I remember and felt clearly my small body, the cold, the hunger and the fear. I died quickly. I do not know how, but I let go, and then was in a realm of peace and colour.

Two months later, a meditation gave me this experience:

My first impressions were unclear but, suddenly, I saw myself watching a little girl, from a rich family, playing and dancing with friends in a garden. She had brown curly hair, was very pretty and wore a pink petticoat and small boots.

I was sad, because I did not belong and was standing in a corner. I was dressed in a simple, blue and white cotton dress, with a Holland cap, admiring the little girl. I have no recollection of what happened next, or to me. However, I saw a lake—or was it a river?—nearby, and I was floating in it at the end.

Two years later, another past life:

As soon as I entered the tunnel into this past life, a terrible fear crept over me and I started crying. Even though I could not see anything, I felt a pain coming through my feet. I was terrified, but could not scream. I suffered a horrific fate.

This was the ending of a life. I was condemned for some ill-deed that I had not committed. When the pain became unbearable, I fainted and left my body. I could see all the people standing around who had accused and misjudged me, leading to my suffering this early death.

My question had been whether this was a connection to France, or to any person in my life, but I could not find out. I assume that this was a burning at the stake, because the flames came up my feet first. Forgiving my accusers was done with tears and sadness.

One short meditation showed me that I had been a sister of a Protestant Nursing Order, wearing their black costume with a white vestment. I could not find out whether there were any connections to people in this life. However, I gave birth in a hospital that was lead by Diakonissen, Sisters of a Protestant nursing order.

Another short meditation showed me that I had been living in Norway, in the Fjord area. We were living in a fishing village in simple homes. The village was located near the sea, in very rough surroundings and close to nature. It looked like the Vikings. I seem to have been female.

In one of my meditations, I found myself standing on a cliff, overlooking a bay. I was looking for a boat or ship, which I could not see. But I knew it was there, as this was the reason I was standing there. Maybe I wanted to wave goodbye to it, or to someone.

I was a middle-aged woman, dressed in a white tunic like the Roman women used to wear, with the material of the tunic held together on the shoulders with a brooch.

My feelings were blocked. I asked questions, but no answers came. I felt sad and disappointed. I did not go close to the cliff so as to avoid being seen.

I had to think of Dido and Aeneas, whose story had touched me so much during my Latin course. Dido killed herself when Aeneas left her to return to his homeland.

Two years later, another meditation:

I was a proud owner of large areas of land. There was a castle, fortress-like. It was in Germany or England. I kept everything ship-shape, was very particular and demanded a lot from my servants and workers. I was dressed in stylish clothes and wore boots, like nobility. I had a whip with me for my horse, but there was no horse to be seen. There was a large courtyard with buildings around.

I died in my own large bed, with people around me. I could not make out whether these people were family or servants.

I asked for forgiveness for my harsh treatment of dependents, and forgave all who hurt me.

In my last meditation, I saw myself as a schoolgirl with pigtails. I wore a long dress and high leather boots. I was standing in a beautiful autumn-coloured forest. Many coloured leaves adorned the ground.

My feelings were numb and I could not find out anything else.

When dying, I was still a child.

12. Insights into My Past Lives

My experiences during meditations helped me to overcome many problems in this life. Depending on our own choices during our life; depending on how we handle challenges and problems, whether positively or negatively, we also facilitate our ending.

It is imperative that we solve all the given tasks in life, no matter how hard they are, because they help us to progress to a higher level of development. There is no way of quitting life before the God-given time. If we try to avoid difficult lessons, try to suicide out of life, we will have to come back into another life where we will have to face the same dilemma all over. Before birth, we have decided to take on our life's challenges, and a promise is a promise before God.

Beyond that, I found out that people in this life have also been in other lives with me. The reward was to know that we all meet again, somewhere in time, when it all fits in with the Universal wisdom. Whether we have a good life, are rich or poor, all depends on the past and on what is on our slate; the Akashic, or Universal record. It is cause and effect.

We are learning to feel the hurt we have inflicted on others. Many illnesses are the result of serious ill-deeds done, to people or animals in a former life, and are sometimes incurable. The eyes of God are everywhere.

13. Leaving the Bush

In 2002, I moved to a little town on the Mid North Coast where I had found a house that suited me. When I moved in, I found out that the house stood on underwater lines. It was too late to change.

Underwater lines are detrimental to health. Spirits that are earth-bound, and have not gone to the light, are attracted to underwater lines. The spirits were there. Every morning, they produced the smell of cooked porridge. A medium helped to exorcise six ghosts, though they were reluctant to leave. Five of the ghosts had died of illnesses, the sixth had his throat cut while in a human body.

Despite the efforts of the medium, the smell continues to this day. I just let them be. They do not bother me. I have my house checked by a Feng Shui professional yearly, for more positive energy. The neighbourhood is unfriendly, but I have found some friends further away.

14. Visions

My love of books and reading continues. I found Paramahansa Yogananda's *Autobiography of a Yogi*. A card inside offered a magazine from the Self-Realisation Fellowship, in the US. When it arrived, I found a picture of Jesus in it. It fascinated me. I could not get my eyes off his face—it somehow came alive. Jesus' eyes looked at me intensely. Tears were running down my face and a warm, loving feeling came over me. I felt embraced with love. It felt wonderful. I framed the picture and it is always with me, but it never again became alive. I have seen his face in visions again.

Still, this was a big event for me. I took it as a sign from above, as I did when I had seen the first colours with my third eye.

Thereafter, I had visions on and off. I often took a short rest in the afternoon, falling asleep quickly, and would be woken by beautiful pictures. These were often golden, with green or purple; in particular a golden, friendly face of an elderly man with a beard. At other times, and quite often, I saw a large golden eye in a living face. At different times, I saw a white rose, a daisy, a pansy, a brown horse and a mountain path with a long road ahead. I could not follow it, because the vision disappeared. There are very intense loving feelings connected with these visions. When I open my eyes, tears are running down my face. I have never experienced these feelings on any previous occasion.

One afternoon, I woke up with the following vision:

I saw myself sitting in bed, with my huge, guardian angel behind me, enfolding me from behind with his oversized body and arms. I practically lay on him/her. He/she was beautiful, everything golden, as were several other angels sitting around my bed. All of them were huge. I opened my eyes with tears running down my face. A wonderful feeling of love overwhelmed me. I felt so happy. Unfortunately, after opening my eyes, I could not see my angels any more.

At another relaxed break in the afternoon, I saw a vision with an angel. Up in the sky, surrounded by a ball of white light, I could see within it a beautiful female figure; an angel in a long silvery dress. It looked magnificent. I wished at that moment that I could paint.

Maybe, some painters have this kind of vision and are then able to save these beautiful images on canvas.

The next vision was of a cross of white light, with a half-figure of Jesus showing through. The view changed, so that I saw Jesus and then the cross behind him, or I saw the cross before Jesus. It was the Jesus whose picture I have framed, standing in my bedroom.

These visions turn up unexpectedly and always overwhelm me. I may feel spirits around me. Also, I notice if they send me a perfume that I can identify with a family member or friend. However, I cannot see them.

There are some exceptions, though: I have seen an animal that had died. One of my cats had suffered a stroke. He had been very dear to me and, as I knew the signs of a stroke, I had him put to sleep. A few days after his death, I saw him walking in front of me, just for a few seconds. Then he was gone. He said 'hello', showing me that he was well again and alive.

Sometimes, departed cats come at night, walking on my bedding, kneading with their front paws. I can feel their movements, but cannot see them. On and off, I may see the shadow of an animal in my house. As I found out, departed animals often stay around in the home in which they used to live. They also visit their former animal friends, and talk to them.

I believe, strongly, that people from the realm of heaven visit us regularly, on certain days when we think of them, because of birthdays or wedding anniversaries. If we still lovingly remember them, they will also remember us.

I am very sure that I have an angel or spirit looking over my shoulder while I am writing. They seem to help with ideas, with corrections and with finding missing words. This is very helpful to me.

Some mornings, I awoke with poems in my head. I wrote them down. They were perfect and did not need any corrections. I do not remember whether I worked on them while asleep, because I read that we all leave our bodies during sleep, to visit our departed loved ones. I just took them as they came.

Once, I received a gift of a book, by Diana Cooper, titled *Angel Inspiration*, from a girlfriend. It introduced me towards finding a new way to involve angels in my life. I knew about our guardian angel being with us always, but I did not know his/her name. I found out the name of my angel.

Angels are very helpful, if we ask them nicely, and a 'thank you' afterwards is appreciated. When I have lost something, He will point out to me where I have mislaid the object. Many times, when driving in a crowded area, I ask for a parking spot and, though it may sound suspicious, most of the time there is suddenly one for us to stop the car in. Angels are huge entities. They have the wisdom of heaven and can see the wider, universal picture.

If I need an emotional boost, because I feel low, I imagine my angel holding me, comforting my inner child. Really, we are never alone, even if it feels like it; spirits and angels guide us all the time.

15. My search brought results

On my long way to maturity, I learned by trial and error. I needed to know what is important for me in my life. Everybody needs love, and we have to give it to each other unconditionally.

Everybody needs acceptance for the way he/she is. We need to respect that we are all different, and have grown up in family circles under a variety of conditions.

Accepting other people and situations as they are is not easy, because we perceive the happenings around us with emotions attached to them. Unless we learn to control our emotions, it may be difficult to achieve peace of mind.

As Shakespeare wrote:

"Life is a stage on which we all have our role to play".

If we become aware of our role in life, we may find a way 'to live happily ever after'.

Life is as happy as we make it ourselves. No one else can make us happy. It is up to our moods and feelings. Some say laughter is the best medicine; others suggest that humour softens the blow in any difficult situation. We may have to find out which suits us best.

We can achieve anything, if we put our mind to it, so it is important to maintain a positive mindset. Negative thinking leads us to negative outcomes.

I am grateful for all the obstacles I encountered on my life-path, because they forced me to learn to find a way to remove them. The constant knocks stopped me from resting on my laurels, because I always knew that more knocks were just around the corner. It took many years until I could incorporate this notion, and learned to handle these hiccups better. Life is not a merry-go-round, instead it's a roller-coaster ride: every day has its Ups and Downs.

I can honestly say I am blessed to know, and to have known, so many loving persons who helped me along my life-path. I would have liked to have been without a few uncomfortable persons, but these people also taught me lessons I needed to learn. Life did not turn out as I had wished it when I was young. The Universal Mind had other plans for me. Nonetheless, I am happy with the result.

Desiderata

Go placidly amid the noise and haste, and remember what peace there may be in silence.

As far as possible without surrender be on good terms with all persons. Speak your truth quietly and clearly; and listen to others, even the dull and ignorant; they too have their story. Avoid loud and aggressive persons: they are vexations to the spirit. If you compare yourself with others, you may became vain and bitter; for always there will be greater and lesser persons than yourself. Enjoy your achievements as well as your plans. Keep interested in your own career, however humble; it is a real possession in the changing fortunes of time. Exercise caution in your business affairs; for the world is full of trickery. But let this not blind you to what virtue there is; many persons strive for high ideals; and everywhere life is full of heroism. Be yourself. Especially, do not feign affection. Neither be cynical about love; for in the face of all aridity and disenchantment it is perennial as the grass. Take kindly the counsel of the years, gracefully surrendering the things of youth. Nurture strength of spirit to shield you in sudden misfortune. But do not distress yourself with imaginings. Many fears are born of fatigue and Loneliness. Beyond a wholesome discipline, be gentle with yourself. You are a child of the universe, no less than the trees and the stars; you have a right to be here. And whether or not it is clear to you, no doubt the universe is unfolding as it should. Therefore be at peace with God, whatever you conceive Him to be, and whatever your labours and aspirations in the noisy confusion of life keep peace with your soul. With all its sham, drudgery and broken dreams, it is still a beautiful world. Be careful. Strive to be happy.

Found in Old Saint Paul's Church. Baltimore; dated 1692

References

Trance Healer by Pat O'Neill and his cassettes;
Spiritual teacher Ilse Kohl, Hamilton-North/Newcastle, NSW;
Astrology teacher Willi Grabau, Newcastle, NSW.
Soul Search by Glen Williston & Judith Johnstone;
The Other Side - an account of my experience with psychic phenomena by James Albert Pike with Diane Kennedy;
Soulmates by Jess Stearn;
Past Lives and present relationships by John van Auken;
You can heal your life by Louise L. Hay;
Professional help by Don Steadman, Kotara/Newcastle, NSW;
The Game of Life, The Power of the spoken Word, Your Word is your Wand, The Secret of Success all by Florence Scovel Shinn;
Past Lives, present dreams by Denise Linn and her cassette series;
There is a River by Thomas Sugrue;
Reincarnation - Claiming your past, creating your future by Lynn Elwell Sparrow;
Edgar Cayce on Reincarnation by Noel Langley;
Many Mansions and *The World Within* by Gina Cerminara;
Second Sight by Edmund Harold;
Angel Inspirations by Diana Cooper;
Betty Shine: Mind to Mind, her Workbook and others;
Aron Abrahamsen *On Wings of Spirit - A life guided to discover spiritual gifts*;
James Redfield: *The Celestine Prophecy*;
The Tenth Insight and *An Experiential Guide* with Carol Adrienne;
Books by Stuart Wilde, Wayne Dyer, Ruth Montgomery and Shirley Maclaine;
Neale Donald Walsch: *Conversation with God, 1, 2 and 3*;
Peace Pilgrim: Her life and Work in her own words
and others.

Acknowledgements

I would like to express my gratitude for the help I received with corrections on my English grammar by a dear friend and teacher in Bulahdelah, Marie Smith, recently passed on; and for the same reason to David Fry, former pharmacist in Kempsey, who took the time to correct my English in this story with dedication and thoughtfulness before I felt confident enough to send it to the publisher.

I was lucky to have known Ilona Wohlgemuth who believed in me ever since we met in 1985 until her early death, and feel very grateful to our mutual friend Anna Akerman who encouraged and supported me when I doubted my abilities to finish this job.

On my long road to the end it was also Rosie Sutherland from Paper Horse Design & Publishing who surprised me after reading my story, saying, that she liked it.

I feel like running away

I feel like running away,
away from all human connections,
away from civilisation
with it's false intentions,
it's unfaithful living and
corrupt behaviour towards nature.

I feel the need to dissolve my being
with nature itself
to become the ground I stand on,
to grow into the tall tree
that shelters me,
to bloom like the wild flower,
to develop into a seed
to rejuvenate into new living.

I need to feel the Oneness with the Universe
close to my heart –
to understand God's need to create human beings,
to understand the intelligence in us,
to create marvellous inventions,
and still commit the most horrific deeds and crimes
no animal would ever do.

Animals seem to be the highest evolved species on earth,
while human beings are the undeveloped ego of Satan
who used to be an angel
but would never obey God's laws.
Humans still have not learned to obey God's laws,
still strive to be Gods themselves.
We did not evolve much ever
since the first brother murder.
We haven't changed at all –
How long ago was it that God created Adam and Eve?

I feel a need to going home
to God –
to find peace at the other end of life –
to learn the higher order of
understanding, tolerance, patience,
and learn to acknowledge the difference
between myself and other souls.

I feel being uprooted
from earthly living.
I need to get away
from close encounters with people.
I need to build my island
to find peace again within me.
May God be my shepherd
to lead me to green pastures
and spring waters –
May the Lord be my shepherd.

That was it

The romantic dream of a marriage and family life
had dissipated into nothingness,
into a broken dream.
What was left?
Dissolution, emptiness,
the end of a bumpy road.

There I stood at the cross road.
Which way was I to go?

At first there was an inner search
for meaning of it all,
an uncertain tapping in the dark
until the fog of negativity and darkness had lifted:
There could be a new beginning!

Time and daily duties are wonderful healers.
Even the deepest wound will be covered
with new skin after a while,
will integrate,
and the pain will disappear completely.
A thought and memory of the hurt
could be tucked away,
somewhere deep inside,
it need not be touched, ever.

Then there would be room for a new beginning.
The mind will see the silver lining around the cloud:
Today was to be lived and enjoyed.
The future, tomorrow has new dreams.
Suddenly, the road ahead looked bright and clear.

Romantic love

Romantic love is an illusion
of love not of this plane,
a longing for a perfect togetherness
of two souls in unity
with deep emotions,
giving of and to each other
in complete harmony,
body, mind, spirit and soul.
Romantic love is a mind creation.
It lives within a halo of uniqueness,
idealised in a dream state,
remembered by our soul
from the experience in different dimensions,
between lives.
It is this longing for the unconditional love
immersed on that special soul.
This cannot be realised on this earth plane.
Romantic love on earth
may become a habit forming relationship,
may destroy many of the illusions
about that idealised partner.
It could also evolve into a mature partnership,
with understanding, respect and
never ending unconditional love.

Memories are forever

Memories are forever
but they may put hooks into the mind
spoiling the present
if past events are idealised.
Memories are moments
in one's life,
experiences,
which help to grow
into the future
with a richer understanding.
We all have memories
on which we built our lives,
either based on anger, resentment and disappointment,
loving memories can brighten up
the spirit of a person,
encouraging optimism,
happiness and success.
All memories have to be outgrown
at one point in time
to make room for the new.
Even though memories are building blocks
they also become tattered and worn,
like old shoes,
and eventually have to be discarded.
Only a glimmer
of some special glory
from years ago
stays in a romantic version
in our minds, forever
to dream and fantasise about
in old age.

I *feel free* -

As the birds in the air,
As the fish in the sea.

I feel free –
To be like the wind
I follow my spirit, my heart.

I feel free –
I release my guilt and fear.
The past is forgiven.
I am free in the Now.

I feel free –
I believe in myself –
I trust my inner knowing.

I feel free –
To live
To love –
To enjoy life.

I am one with the Universe.

Uniform

Uniform the minds –
uniform the nations –
uniform the races –
uniform religions.

Groups –
sports to non sports –
class to class –
rich to poor –
young to old.

When we arrive from heaven
we are connected to all –
in love, harmony and peace.

On earth we are ripped apart from all
by uniformed, grouped minds,
brought up to fight,
to ignore, condemn and judge,
to hate and destroy.

There is hope
in the free spirit of our minds –
shedding conditioning –
leaving behind the clutter of society,
uniforms and groups,
thinking feelingly with the heart –
with enthusiasm and universal love
in harmony and with peace.

www.ingramcontent.com/pod-product-compliance
Lightning Source LLC
Chambersburg PA
CBHW032011040426
42448CB00006B/580